DEVELOP YOUR PSYCHIC ABILITY

Unlock your intuition and psychic potential

DEVELOP YOUR PSYCHIC ABILITY

*Unlock your intuition
and psychic potential*

Hazel Whitaker

METRO BOOKS
NEW YORK

CONTENTS

CONTENTS

INTRODUCTION

AS WE APPROACH THE NEW MILLENNIUM, THERE IS AN INCREASING CURIOSITY ABOUT THE BEST AND SIMPLEST METHODS OF DEVELOPING OUR PERSONAL PSYCHIC ABILITY.

In this age of new awareness about psychic power, the multiple benefits of such knowledge becomes increasingly obvious. We are all motivated to develop our powers of perception and intuition, recognizing their quality and value as we strive to achieve our personal goals. Your mental powers, such as intuition, are heightened during the process of psychic development, and this gives you greater power over your own destiny.

You will discover that the exercises involved also heighten your other five senses. This creates a happy energy that not only benefits yourself, but reaches out to those whose destinies you also encounter and affect. All goals require effort and commitment. Victory comes from daring to begin.

The exercises and meditation formulas described in this book are designed to aid you in your psychic development. They are precise and easy to comprehend. You will discover how to increase your telepathic skills and develop skills in clairvoyance, cards, psychometry, palmistry and astral travel. You will learn the advantages of meditation, such as how to relax the body and mind, and how to focus. You will also become aware of the importance of protecting yourself from negative influences.

Poor choices in personal relationships can have a devastating impact on your life with long-term side effects. How many times have you had to ask yourself: "Why didn't I listen to my intuition?" — once the damage had been done. Psychic development trains you to listen to and respect your intuition. How much easier it would be to make the right decisions and choices, in advance, about important aspects of your life — you can, if you are armed with advanced intuitive instinct.

Have you ever wondered about your child's fantasies? You can learn how to recognize the difference between your child's fantasies and his or her early psychic awareness without causing the child alarm. And the ability to communicate with loved ones who have passed over, while an awesome experience, will give you peace of mind.

This book will also show you how to become aware of and then to acknowledge your guardian angel, or spirit guide as some people prefer to call it. This book will show you your guardian angel's purpose in your life, and how to build up a mutual relationship of trust with it.

While you can successfully practice all the exercises described in this book by yourself, you will discover the benefits of joining a psychic workshop or creating your own. You will come to understand auras and how to cleanse them. You will also discover what separates the fine line between coincidence, intuition and psychic phenomena, and how they all form part of the concept of your innate psychic ability. This book will also explain to you the importance of knowing when it is appropriate to use your psychic ability and when it is not.

But before you proceed with developing your psychic ability, you should realize that there is no room for self-doubt or fear in this mission. These two negative emotions feed on each other, interrupting the flow of positive energy which you should be dedicated to building if you are to succeed. We often fear what we do not fully understand, but we may never truly understand all that we are capable of if we allow fear to create its barrier.

There are many advantages in developing your psychic ability, such as easier communication between yourself and other people, an affinity with animals, and the ability to sense danger thereby avoiding it. The peace of mind and personal happiness which are the result of a deeper understanding of self will be the ultimate reward for your effort.

WHAT IS PSYCHIC ABILITY

TO UNDERSTAND THE NOTION OF PSYCHIC PHENOMENA YOU NEED TO REALIZE THAT THE MIND IS A POWERFUL VEHICLE OF COMMUNICATION. IT REQUIRES ITS OPERATOR TO MAKE USE OF ITS FULL POTENTIAL AND THIS OPERATOR MUST ALWAYS BE YOURSELF.

Coincidence or Intuition?

You might be wondering what the differences are between instinct, intuition or E.S.P. (extra sensory perception) and coincidence. Many notable events are attributed to coincidence. Things happen simply by chance, or so it seems, but in many of these instances our instincts have propelled us to be in a certain place at a certain time or have detained or prevented us from being at a place where we had intended to be. The result of these coincidences can be profound; for instance, how often have you heard someone sigh with relief because some unexpected circumstance caused them to miss a journey that ended in disaster? Then there are those people whose lives have been changed — career paths, lovers, bank balances — simply because they happened to be in the right place at the right time. Some might say that these occurrences are coincidence. Sometimes, these events are just too strange and too significant to be dismissed that easily.

Psychic Ability

The person who is able to accurately predict world events or see into the secrets and intimate experiences of people they have never seen before are referred to as psychics — a collective term for people who can see, hear or feel significant incidents with clarity, either through advanced psychic awareness or with the aid of a medium such as Tarot cards, a crystal ball, tea leaf reading, or other ritualistic devices.

By developing your own psychic ability you will discover which of these disciplines most suits you, for this will be the one you will go on to perfect.

Science and the Psychic

Science does not accept very easily that which it cannot measure. Psychical research has gone on now for over 100 years. The Soviet Union took a particular interest in it, as has the United States of America. While there is a great deal of circumstantial evidence to support its existence, when scientists take reputedly accurate psychics into the laboratory, they find that their experiments prove not much more conclusive than coincidence. What scientists do not take into account is that psychic ability is not something that can operate effectively under laboratory conditions. The tests are uninteresting and meaningless. Psychics are very effective when dealing with matters of importance, either to the world or to an individual.

Scientists continue to probe for logical and practical explanations to psychic phenomena. This is in itself an acknowledgment of its probable existence — after all, you don't investigate a crime that never happened nor an event that never took place.

Psychic phenomenon is not tangible. Since it does not come from the material world, trying to find answers from physical sources will always prove fruitless.

Throughout history, psychic phenomenon has had its fair share of critics who have condemned and ridiculed it, but just as you cannot intimidate a true believer, you will never convince a nonbeliever of its existence.

We are fortunate to live in a time when our desires for psychic awareness and personal development can be assisted by the vast amount of knowledge accumulated by those who have studied and experienced this mysterious phenomena. It is this New Age mentality that encourages us to seek, until we find, our inner selves, to defy tunnel vision, and to become the very best that we can be without fear of ridicule.

The Advantages of Psychic Development

Few people embark on a journey of exploration into the unknown without knowledge of its advantages and disadvantages. All knowledge is not necessarily good knowledge, but all good knowledge should be valued. Psychic development delivers valuable knowledge about reaching your full potential for both spiritual and material evolvement.

When all your senses, including your sixth sense — intuition or in its more powerful form E.S.P. — are working to their fullest capacity, there will be little you cannot achieve through effort and commitment to the task at hand. There will be fewer dangers to encounter because you are now able to sense negative energy in people and places. In your personal relationships, you will be less likely to choose a wrong mate, for you will now listen to that little voice that tells you he or she is no good for you.

Important career choices are usually made based on practical and logical reasons. This is commendable, except when your intuition is trying to warn you. If this happens, you need to take into account how your decision will affect your personal life. Happy people produce happy results; unhappy people tend to become ineffective over time and cause themselves and others distress.

Communication is the key to solving most of life's problems. Learning good communication skills is a part of psychic development.

Animals — Communication and Spirit Entities

Communicating with nature and animals requires only the belief that it is possible to do so, as anyone with an animal companion will tell you. The highly developed intuition possessed by animals goes beyond communicating with people and other animals — your animal companion can perceive the presence of spirit entities. You will know when this is happening, because the hair on its back stands on end. The animal becomes agitated and appears to want to attack the invisible presence — but then it will become calm though still focused on the space occupied by the entity. You can now know that an entity is in the room, and where. This gives you the opportunity to communicate directly with this spirit visitor. As an advanced psychic you will also be able to encourage those lost souls to find the light that will bring them peace.

ARE YOU PSYCHIC?

EVERYONE INTERESTED IN PSYCHIC PHENOMENA WONDERS IF THEY ARE PSYCHIC. ALMOST EVERYBODY HAS THE POTENTIAL TO INCREASE HIS OR HER PSYCHIC ABILITY. THE EXCEPTIONS ARE THOSE WHO FEAR ITS POWER AND THEREFORE REJECT IT, OR THOSE WHO REFUSE TO ACKNOWLEDGE ITS EXISTENCE.

People with psychic ability have always been around, in tribal societies, advanced ancient civilizations, as well as our own highly technical world. Intuition, E.S.P., telepathy, clairvoyance, clairaudience, spiritualism, psychic healing, card reading, crystal gazing, and tea leaf reading, among other skills, are individual and collective disciplines that come under the umbrella of psychic phenomena. You can learn any one of these or all of them if you have the desire and the patience.

How many times have you known who is calling you when the phone rings? Have you ever woken from a deep sleep or stopped in your tracks, alarmed because you felt a loved one was in danger? If any of these things have happened to you, then you have the potential for psychic development.

There are many simple tests in the following chapters with which to test your psychic potential and your progress, but first of all you must believe in yourself and commit to the task you have set for yourself. Of course there are people who seem to be born with a highly developed psychic ability and most of those go on to become very useful to people in all aspects of their lives.

People who see, hear or feel impressions concerning events and circumstances of which they have no previous knowledge are known as psychics. If this is who you wish to be, much of your time and energy should be devoted to the study of psychic ability and psychic-enhancing exercises.

Recognizing the Early Stages of Psychic Awareness

Exploration of personal psychic ability in the early stages of awareness requires only simple detective exercises. Sometimes, psychics are referred to as "sensitives". This theory stems from the belief that in some degree or another we are all sensitive to the energy fields around us. Have you ever felt a distinct chill in the air while you have been in a warm building? Unlike the chill you feel when you are running a fever, a psychic chill is usually accompanied by an eerie feeling that disappears once you vacate the scene.

There is another example of sensing energies around you that is very common and negative. This energy comes from people known as "psychic leaches" or "vampires". Is there someone in your life who demands a great deal from you? Do you feel drained and weak after a lengthy session with this person? If the answers to these questions are "Yes", you have a problem. Psychic leaches suck the energy from other people's auras without even being aware that they are doing so. If you are plagued in this manner, it is important to ask yourself if you are really doing this person any good, because there are many people who will not be bothered sorting out their own problems. There are two solutions to this situation. You can ask your guardian angel (see THE IMPORTANCE OF GUARDIAN ANGELS, page 36) to put a shield of protection around your aura (see *Psychic Shields* on page 40), or you can encourage that person not to be so reliant on you. As you progress with your psychic development, you will learn how to cleanse and shield your aura from these intrusions.

Whenever you think you are picking up energies from the atmosphere, record these impressions as they happen. This exercise not only strengthens your faith in your psychic ability, it will actually sharpen it.

Combining E.S.P. with the sense of touch is an excellent way to practice and develop psychic ability. It could also lead to developing skills in the area of psychic healing (see pages 62–65). Naturally these skills are not supposed to compete with those of orthodox medicine; they are a way of helping you help yourself to heal with your doctor's approval.

How Luke Discovered His Psychic Ability

Luke was only eleven years old when he came to me for advice about the strange new experiences that were causing him anxiety and confusion. It all started during a conversation he was having with a school friend about football. He explained that he had a sudden, strange, tight feeling in the pit of his stomach, followed by a strong impression of danger for his friend. His gut feeling was telling him to warn his friend not to go to football practice that evening. "You're going to get hurt," he warned his friend. "Yeah, sure," his friend replied. "You're just jealous because you didn't make the team."

Luke knew this wasn't true because he didn't like football — he had only applied to be on the team to please his father, but his friend didn't believe him. The next day, when Luke's friend was absent from school, he was told that his friend had suffered a head injury during football practice the previous evening. Luke was spooked and asked his mother to take him to visit his friend. His friend accused Luke of having caused the accident to happen.

This was by no means Luke's only psychic experience. He was able to relate more stories which always began with the peculiar tummy sensation followed by an intuitive impression concerning an event connected to the person he was with. Fortunately the news he receives is not always bad — he also foresees happy events. I told him that just because you receive a message for someone, this does not always mean that you must pass the message on. If you listen closely to your intuition it will tell you which messages are best kept to yourself.

Psychic ability is not a power game, but can be a powerful advantage. When one so young as Luke has psychic experiences it can cause alarm and confusion for all concerned. Loving guidance and understanding is absolutely necessary in the early stages of psychic development. Luke is a little older now and is no longer intimidated by his psychic ability.

Psychic Messages versus Coincidence

When something odd happens, but which at the same time is meaningful, logical people will say: "That was just a coincidence." A example of this happens to many people and is so common that there is a term for it: "book fairy". Have you ever gone into a bookshop looking for a book on a particular subject and while you were wandering the aisles, a book on a completely unrelated subject either falls from the shelf in front of you or is brought to your attention in an equally unusual way? The book proves to provide answers to a dilemma you were having or benefits you in some other way that matters. When the book fairy is at work, logical people cannot find a tangible explanation for how this important book is suddenly in their hands. This is why coincidence is a such a key word in their vocabulary.

Psychic messages regarding emotional issues such as love, romance and family ties are very often the hardest to interpret. Psychic messages come in many forms, coincidence is just one of them. Dreams, papers being blown off a desk that reveal something to you, items being knocked over that draws your attention to something, are just a few of the ways that a psychic message might come to you. This could be your guardian angel trying to get a message through to you.

First Encounter with a Guardian Angel

During your period of meditation in a psychic workshop you could have your first encounter with a guardian angel. Communication with the spirit world is an exciting part of psychic development. But too much excitement will create a barrier. You need to calm down, so meditate until you can maintain a level of tranquillity which will then allow you access to this encounter.

Your guardian angel will be pleased that you have eventually made contact. Until you are used to this process, you could have difficulty hearing with clarity the detail of the intended messages. Until a stage of ease and tranquillity is achieved, a mixture of muffled sounds, part words and partial sentences are more likely to be the result of these early experiences.

Time, patience and practice are essential now. This way you will receive clear and distinctive messages instead of muffled mixed sounds and signals.

Fear

Fear is the number one setback to any form or degree of psychic ability. It is an emotional force which is necessary to acknowledge and respect because it warns us of danger. However, it must be controlled and should never totally govern our decisions, choices and actions.

To fear something or someone because you do not fully understand the person or concept is negative and self-destructive. This kind of fear can become phobic if you imagine that some superior force will prevent or destroy your personal goals. To fear a tyrannical personality is understandable; but even a tyrant can only intimidate you for as long as you allow him or her to do so for tyrants are only bullies who control and dominate the weak and vulnerable.

Fear originates from a lack of belief and confidence in yourself. Warnings against potentially dangerous activities given to super-sensitive people should always be accompanied by a reasonable explanation as to why, when, where and how to use adequate protection. Otherwise, these sensitive people may confuse worthy challenges with dangerous activities. If this happens, they will be denied the joy of achievement that comes from overcoming fear.

The main cause of failure to commit to psychic development is fear of the unknown. This must be overcome if you are ever to reach your full psychic potential. Fear of the unknown is similar in nature to fear of failure to succeed in relationships or business, and can prevent you from enjoying success.

Superstitious fear is common. The list of superstitions is endless, some examples being: walking under a ladder, lucky seven, black Friday, shoes on a table top, and traveling without a lucky mascot. While it is often treated in a lighthearted manner, superstitious fear does control the activities of many people. The mystery surrounding psychic phenomena attracts even those most fearful of its power. The best cure for fear of the unknown comes from knowledge.

To fear the unknown is to rob the spirit of knowledge
which is the reward of any new experience.

INTUITION

What is Intuition?

Every person is born with the basis of that inner sense we call "intuition". Basic intuition, once trusted, can be developed into E.S.P. or psychic ability. Unfortunately, as we develop the disciplines of "reason" or logic our instincts and intuition are often undermined. A too highly developed sense of logic will shut out instinct and intuition, and thus true insight. Intuition begins with instinct as you will see from the following.

Instinct is a universal gift from nature to all living things; it is the unity of the five senses — seeing, hearing, feeling, tasting and smelling — that is unimpaired by either time or space. Instinct enables organisms to live, to procreate, and to survive. Hippocrates, the 5th-century B.C. Greek philosopher, known as the "father of medicine", wrote: "It is the instinct of the earlier races, when cold reason had not as yet obscured man's inner vision. … Its indication must never be disdained, for it is to instinct alone that we owe our first remedies."

Intuition is your innate knowing that something is so, even in the absence of objective evidence. Intuition immediately reaches into the heart of the matter; it enables you to grasp art, music and beauty, and is at the basis of humankind's desire for knowledge.

Insight is intuiting some truth, being able to make sense of that truth and express that understanding to others. Insight brings a person peace and a flexible certainty that they are perceiving truth. People known for their insight do not allow material arguments (logic) to deter them in their knowledge, whether or not it is reinforced by evidence.

E.S.P. or extrasensory perception is intuition and insight developed to a very high level. It is the awareness of an event or influence without help from material evidence. When a person can intuit an external object, event or influence, he or she is known as clairvoyant. Intuiting the mind of another person is known as telepathy. When a person can "see" into the future, it is called precognition.

How Intuition Works

Every living thing emits energy and energy cannot be destroyed. Know that "thought" is an energy. You experience intuition when you sense one or more sets of energies that come from the energies of a place or from another's thoughts or energy emissions. When someone says: "I'm getting really good vibes about that", they are in fact saying: my intuition is telling me that situation feels right for me.

Some Facts about Intuition

* Intuition is receiving energy in the form of feelings or "vibes" that make you "know" something significant about the person, event, or place associated with it.
* You must never use your mind, your intellect, your sense of reason to analyze your "message", no matter how incongruous or strange it is. If you do, you will contaminate the experience with what you think you know — you intuition will pick up on variables of which you are consciously unaware and which can have significant effects on a person, situation or place.
* You cannot force intuition to happen — you can only open yourself to receive it. The exercise below will help you develop your intuition.

How to Distinguish between Intuition and Your Hopes and Fears

It is most difficult to tell the difference between your intuition and your hopes and fears when you have an emotional investment in the situation or great expectations from it. This is because when we are emotionally involved we tend to stack the evidence in our own favor — this is normal and natural; however, it is not a good position to be in when trying to determine the truth of the matter.

When your intuition is at work, you are conscious of receiving some information that you know to be true. There is a sense of peace or quiet about this knowledge. You can look at it as something that originated from outside yourself. This may cause you distress or great joy, but that sense of quiet is behind whatever other emotions you may experience as a result of the message — in fact, your response would be similar to that on learning something important, and which you know to be true, from another individual.

If your hopes and fears are behind your certainty about something — for instance, "I know John loves me!" (despite the fact that he is about to marry someone else) — you will have a feeling of desperation at the center of your feeling. If we take the same example and your knowing comes from true intuition, there will be no sense of desperation in that knowledge, even though you may feel some desperation because John is marrying someone else — the difference is that you can recognize this desperation as a feeling separate from the original intuitive knowledge.

An Exercise

If you truly wish to know the truth about something in which you have a great deal to lose or gain, breathe in and out, gradually slowing your breathing until you are in a state of mental relaxation. While breathing, starting from the top of your head, focus on relaxing each part of your body. Once in a state of calm, mentally step right back and view the situation as though it were happening to someone else. Whatever you pick up in this state will most likely be truth, the knowledge gained from your intuition.

An Exercise to Develop Your Intuition

The following exercise is a good one to help you develop your intuition because you will not have an emotional investment in any of the feelings you may pick up.

Choose a sunny day, one that is not too hot or too cold, and go and sit in a park. Choose a time of day when some people will be sitting on the grass, in groups or by themselves, and others are walking by. Practice a meditation exercise, such as the one on page 55, or breathe slowly, deeply, and evenly until you are feeling loose, physically and mentally. You should now be conscious of bird sounds, traffic, people's voices, but you are detached from them all.

Now, allow yourself to be aware of the people around you and those who are wandering by. Remember, you can't order intuitive messages to come to you, you just need to be open to receive them. While you may pick up many faint intuitive messages, there will probably be at least one that you would like to focus on, thus strengthening it. You may receive these messages as feelings or as factual knowledge. You may receive them in your solar plexus or through your "third eye" in the center of your forehead. The physical feeling you get from your intuition is very personal, but it could feel like a sense of excitement, anticipation or unease.

Many intuitive messages can be quite abstract, so if you pick up something, quietly and calmly ask yourself some questions:

* What does the experience feel like? Good? Bad? Happy? Sad? Excited? Anticipation? Bitter?
* Has it affected my mood? For instance, do I feel sudden depression or sudden joy that was not mine to begin with?
* Does it leave almost as quickly as it came, for instance, once the person has passed by? Or does it linger? If so, for how long?

While you are sitting in the park, you will no doubt encounter a few passersby who will engage you in casual conversation. You will very likely enjoy these encounters; however, if you should suddenly feel uneasy, afraid, chilled or nauseous for no apparent reason, and despite the friendly overtures being made by the other person, you could safely assume that your intuition has kicked in.

Key Words
It will help to make a list of key words that will best describe the impressions you receive during this exercise, such as "natural", "unusual", "uneasy", "exciting", "frightening", "sad" and "joyful", which are identified and noted — preferably in a journal — shortly after the experience. Then make a further list of the words: "who", "what", "where", "when", "how" and "why", to explain to yourself the entire experience, keeping in mind that you are dealing with your reactions to the experience.

IS YOUR CHILD PSYCHIC?

ALL CHILDREN FANTASIZE. THEY PLAY GAMES WITH IMAGINARY FRIENDS, AND THEY HAVE CONVERSATIONS WITH THEIR TOYS THAT ARE AS REAL AND AS NATURAL AS SPEAKING TO THEIR PARENTS. SOMETIMES, HOWEVER, A CHILD WILL COME OUT WITH SOMETHING SO EXTRAORDINARY THAT IT CAN NO LONGER BE PUT DOWN TO ORDINARY MAKE-BELIEVE.

"Is my child psychic?" is a question I have been asked many times by concerned parents. The parents come to me because the child has been relating a number of psychic experiences to them, which for the child are perfectly natural events. When the child asks: "Am I psychic?" it is usually because of the parent's amazed reaction.

Fact or Fantasy

There is a difference between psychic experience and normal fantasy. Children fantasize as a natural part of their growing up. Parents are often amused by the exchange of fantasies between children and will sometimes even participate. To the child who is relating a fantasy, his or her account of what happened is as real as the psychic child's experience. The difference between the two is perhaps most easily seen in the consistency of detail in the telling and the retelling. When a child is relating a psychic experience he or she is both persistent and consistent in the account of what happened, whereas the child relating a fantasy is inconsistent about detail and the fantasy is soon forgotten.

Your Reaction

Many children will have imaginary friends. These "friends" are usually put down to fantasy — sometimes, however, the invisible friends are real. Children take their psychic experiences for granted, believing that if they can see visitors from the other side or know events in advance, then so can everyone else. It would be desirable if this ease of being doesn't change. Your reaction will have a great deal to do with what happens next.

Imagine if your child were to suddenly tell you he or she has a new friend and describes someone that you recognize as a long-deceased relative or someone whose name and appearance accurately describe someone from another culture to which your child has had no access. You could find yourself unnerved, even frightened.

If your reaction frightens the child a cycle of fear, anger, repression and suppression could begin. This would be a great pity, as there are other more positive ways to deal with this situation.

Fear of Ridicule

When a parent or other significant adults show fear or disapproval, the child tries to stop the psychic process. The child becomes secretive and withdrawn, shrouded by guilt, until he or she is drawn to another psychic person who understands his or her condition. The fact is, that no matter how hard a parent might strive to drive this tendency underground it will not and cannot be destroyed.

Samantha was 15 years old before she sought the advice of a professional psychic to help her deal with her own psychic ability. She had been feeling so wretched that she just wanted the psychic to make it all go away. Samantha had been having psychic experiences since she was seven years old, but the last five to six years had not been happy ones.

During the early years of her psychic experiences, Samantha had no problems with her ability to predict the future and talk to spirits whom she could see with clarity. The trouble began when her father became convinced that she was hallucinating as the result of mental problems. Her mother on the other hand believed that her daughter was possessed by an evil spirit who was trying to take over the girl's life. Samantha's young friends were also divided in their opinion about the cause of her problems, with the exception of one young man who was able to identify with her psychic experiences and their associated problems.

In their misguided effort to protect their daughter from ridicule and being labeled insane or a freak, Samantha's parents took her to doctors and priests and finally to a psychotherapist. Her attitude to all these people was extremely bad and, coupled with her now young and restless mood swings, these efforts resulted in Samantha becoming very depressed and out of control.

Finally, on the advice of her young male friend, she consulted the psychic who managed to make her understand that what was happening to her was not a bad thing, just unusual and special and the manifestation of her highly developed psychic ability. Once she had come to terms with this knowledge, Samantha was able to cope with her special gift and is now a well-adjusted and happy young woman.

How to Deal with Your Psychic Child

You need to show your children that you have the same faith in them as they are expected to have in you, that you trust in them as they trust in you. Remain open to their experiences — do not show alarm, do not condemn, do not judge. You have to show your child that you believe what they're saying to be true and ask them questions about their experiences without being judgmental or controlling, flippant or condescending. Thus you become the student and your child the teacher. There are no complicated techniques. Approach with the same simplicity with which your child approaches life. In the end it all comes down to trust, conversation, and heartfelt communication.

Exploitation

Your child's psychic abilities are a great gift that should never be exploited or suppressed, manipulated or interfered with. In fact, this could even be dangerous. Allow your child's psychic ability to develop naturally, and just simply be there in a supportive way to listen without judgment. After all, this is all your child is asking from you. It is also a good idea to discreetly watch to ensure that no one else is exploiting or manipulating your child. People can be ruthless about exploiting psychic children for his or her own profit.

EXERCISES FOR DEVELOPING YOUR PSYCHIC ABILITY

THE EXERCISES IN THIS CHAPTER CAN BE PRACTICED BY YOURSELF OR WITH A FRIEND IF ANOTHER PERSON IS NEEDED. PSYCHIC CIRCLES USE THESE EXERCISES, OR ONES LIKE THEM, AT EVERY MEETING.

Testing the Tarot

The Tarot cards provide students of psychic phenomena with ample opportunity for psychic development — in particular the twenty-two cards of the Major Arcana. Each card in the Major Arcana has a descriptive title and is full of symbols all of which have specific meanings. The reader is supposed to study these symbols to further enrich his or her interpretation of the card.

Exercises

At each meeting of a psychic workshop, one of the Major Arcana Tarot cards is passed around the students who are each given a few minutes to examine the picture and explain their immediate impressions. Once all the students have recorded their first impressions, the card is sent on a second round. This time each person is given a little longer to view and interpret the meanings of the card. This procedure is repeated for the interpretation of the card when reversed. It may sound like a long tedious exercise, but I can assure you that I have never met a student of this craft who is not inspired to test his or her intuitive skills by extracting every possible piece of information from the card.

For the purpose of this exercise we will assume that the students have been interpreting card No. VII entitled "The Chariot". The picture reveals an armored soldier steering his chariot. The chariot is drawn by two horses, one white and one black. Everything about the picture suggests that the soldier has perfect control of the vehicle and the horses. In the background we see a picture that suggests affluence — tall stately buildings and lush green fields. The chariot is ornate and curtains decorated by glistening stars adorn the chariot. The soldier wears a crown whose centerpiece is a star. For the benefit of any student who has not been able to interpret the meaning of all these symbols, the teacher will explain both the spiritual and the material meanings of the card:

Spiritual Level: If you are looking for the spiritual enlightenment this card offers, you will see that the message this picture is giving you is that you are the person responsible for the spiritual safety of your vehicle (the soul or conscience). You have been given every advantage to aid you in your safety (represented by the armor and a good pair of horses). The affluence depicted suggests your spiritual guidance is positive. Everything is in your favor for a safe and straight journey through life.

The black and white horses represent the positive and negative forces you must deal with on your journey. If you examine the soldier's face, you will see he is focused on the road ahead. This is the example you must follow if you wish to avoid accidents and setbacks. When this card is in the upright position, it represents the fact that you are taking control of your spiritual life in a safe and orderly fashion.

Reversed it means that you are temporarily out of control. You are travelling in a spiritually damaged vehicle and you are allowing temporary distractions to cause you harm.

Material level: The chariot represents the vehicle you are currently driving such as a bicycle or car. The vehicle is mechanically safe and is capable of being driven in good and bad conditions (the black and white horses). When this card appears in your layout, it suggests you are about to take a journey that is assured of safety and comfort.

Reversed it represents mechanical faults in a car or bicycle that will cause accidents. This card also appears in the reversed position when the driver (you) is proceeding in a careless manner or is under the influence of alcohol or drugs. Either way, it always predicts accidents, but not fatalities.

Summary: All this information, spiritual or material, is contained in this one card. When you review the information, you will see that by concentrating on the picture and extending your intuition it all makes perfect sense. The results of this exercise encourage the student to take the time and effort to develop his or her psychic abilities.

Cut the Cards

Soon you will have advanced enough psychically to move onto the next exercise, for which you will need the twenty-two cards of the Major Arcana. Student John places the cards face down on a tabletop and spreads them out in a fan. Student Sue, using both hands, proceeds to mix the cards around the table, intermingling them while concentrating on a question she wishes to ask, the details of which no other students are told. Sue then gathers up the cards, puts them into a pile and shuffles them. She cuts three packs of cards into three piles with the pictures face down on the table. She turns up each pile face up so that three cards are showing. They are The Lovers, The Chariot and The Moon. She will now try to interpret the meanings associated with the pictures on the cards.

The next step for Sue to learn is how to interconnect the three cards. She starts with the card that takes her immediate attention and ask herself a series of questions. Let's assume that the card is The Lovers. Questions she could ask are: "Is this a good love story or a sad love story?" "Do I feel happy for this couple or do I feel sad?" Then she asks a series of relevant questions for the other two cards.

Sue now has information on the individual cards, but if a story is to be told, these meanings must relate to each other. One of the other two cards is The Chariot, so Sue knows that John is already on the right path to happiness in a loving relationship. The third card is The Moon, which represents fears and phobias. Sue is confused that The Moon has appeared with all the happiness the other cards are predicting. In this case, it is highly probably that The Moon represents some fears and phobias left over from a previous bad relationship experienced by John.

You will enjoy experimenting with your own creative methods of laying out the cards and finding your own intuitive meanings for them. And try to keep records of every interpretation or prediction you make, because at a future date you will want to see how accurate your predictions were.

Astral Travel

Astral travel or out-of-body experiences are the terms used to describe a person's spiritual body leaving the physical body for a period of time and hovering above the physical body or traveling to various places. It is a popular belief of some theorists that the spiritual body is attached to the physical body by a silver-colored cord which has the potential to stretch endlessly during astral travel.

Numerous accounts of these experiences have been studied and are well documented, and they all bear striking similarities. Most out-of-body experiences first happen during a period of unconsciousness or sleep, but many psychically well-developed people can bring them on at will. In a psychic workshop environment students of the out-of-body phenomenon find this part of their psychic development extremely fascinating, and quite often one or two of them are able to identify with the information being discussed. They will then share their personal out of-body experiences in detail with the rest of the group.

In my capacity as a psychic I am frequently approached by people who claim to have had many out-of-body-experiences. Sometimes they reveal a detailed account of an isolated occurrence that might have happened long ago but that they have never been able to forget. Many of the out-of-body experiences related to me have occurred to the person during a period of crisis.

One young man told me that he had been set upon by a gang of thugs who stole from him and beat him unmercifully. He remembered being afraid he was going to die, then suddenly he was outside and above his physical body. When the thugs were finished with the attack, he watched them running away. He found himself following, floating quickly and out of control in midair. Then he heard the sound of an ambulance. When it passed him, he followed it to his body still lying on the sidewalk. He watched the paramedics treating him, then went inside the ambulance with his body. In the hospital emergency room, he saw the medical staff attending to his wounds.

The next thing he remembered was that he woke up, back inside his physical body, seeing his parents consoling him. He now became aware of intense physical pain. He tried to tell his parents about his strange experience, which he knew to be true, and they responded with sympathy

And while their words seemed to be accepting everything he was saying, he could see that their expressions and tone of voice were only meant to humor him. In the years to come, this caused him great stress and frustration. He was now in a situation where he knew he had had an experience and no one believed him. He had to fight to hold onto the truth of his experience, otherwise he would no longer know what was truth and what was not.

You Can Travel Too

Most psychic workshop teachers encourage discussions about the possibility of willful out-of-body-experiences and astral travel. During the period of meditation a student may choose to focus on this subject and visualize his or her astral body leaving the physical body. In this state, he or she will observe the environment, then travel to some place where he or she can observe a scene or activity on which the student later reports in detail.

It is important to remember, however, that it is never acceptable to invade another person's privacy.

An Exercise

When you are learning how to astral travel, there is a very good exercise we have used within the psychic circle with success. While you are in the psychic circle, during the meditation phase, concentrate on a familiar newsstand. Now visualize yourself projecting out of your body and astral traveling along your usual route to the newsstand. Once there, look at the headlines of a newspaper. When you have taken in this information, return to your body in the psychic circle. When you and the group come out of the meditation, report on what you have seen.

Telepathy

Telepathy is a direct mental communication between two people, one of whom is the transmitter and the other the receiver. Pictures, signs, words or sentences can be used by the transmitter to send and be identified by the receiver. Geographical distance will not interfere with the transmission of telepathic messages. While laboratory tests have proved to be inconclusive in proving the power of telepathy, they do identify who is the receiver and who is the transmitter. As is the case with most other methods of psychic communication, real-life experiences offer the more profound evidence.

As an example, some years ago my sisters and I discovered our daughters, then aged 13 and 11 years old, playing a game they called "Guess what?" As they explained it to us at the time, my daughter would conjure up a picture in her mind of some object, person or scene which she "sent" to her cousin's mind. My niece would then interpret the message she was receiving and it was very seldom that she was wrong.

Throughout the years they have periodically tested themselves to see if they are still able to transmit and receive messages from each other by using this method of communication, and indeed they can. The only time they fail the test is when they try to reverse their roles of transmitter and receiver. This suggests that my daughter can only transmit messages, and my niece can only receive them.

In my psychic workshops, we do many tests of this nature. For instance, we place a partition (usually a screen) between two of the students and give one of them a pack of the Major Arcana cards from the Tarot, because their colors and detail are well-defined. The student shuffles the pack, cuts it into two, and places both of them face up, then concentrates on the pictures. Two cards are now showing, and the receiver is then asked to

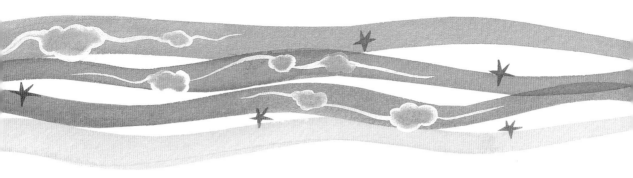

describe them. The more detail they can give about the card, the higher their telepathic power is rated. The students always find this part of their psychic development entertaining as well as useful. It is also fascinating to discover who are the transmitters and who are the receivers. Those who are psychically well developed seem to be able to play either role.

My sister and I had a few good ideas about how our daughters could continue their telepathic games. We called one game "What were you doing on Sunday!" For seven consecutive Sundays my daughter would choose an activity like drawing, skipping or dancing, which she would think of or act out at the specified time of 10:00 a.m. She would then try to transmit the idea to her cousin. At 10:15 a.m. my niece would telephone our house and tell us what she thought my daughter had been doing at 10:00 a.m. Five Sundays out of the seven my niece had guessed correctly.

In another exercise my daughter would take an object belonging to my niece, like a locket or hair comb, and hide it. She would then visualize and transmit the hiding place to my niece, who had to go and find the object. She was successful in finding the object three out of five times.

We even tested the girls' telepathic skills by suggesting that my daughter should try to make her cousin physically do something. For example, my daughter might visualize her cousin standing on a chair in a corner like a naughty child doing time-out. The success rate was about 50 percent in this case. We attributed the fallen success rate to the fact that occasionally my daughter would transmit a deed that she knew her cousin hated doing. Once my daughter tried to will her cousin to make a phone call to a boy that my niece had a crush on. My niece didn't make the call, and this proved to the girls that no one can make you do something you don't want to do.

Basic Psychometry

Jewelry

A piece of jewelry is by far the most popular item offered to a psychic for a psychometry reading, in particular, rings, watches, bracelets and lockets. Even though these items are excellent choices for the novice to practice their psychic skills on, it has to be taken into consideration that some of the predictions may refer to a previous owner. Also, items of jewelry should be placed inside an envelope or other similar container before being handed over. This eliminates the guessing game which can be put into motion by tell-tale signs of the subject's affluence. For instance, an obviously expensive diamond ring will suggest to the psychometrist that the owner is at least financially stable, and this may not be true; but hints of this sort are tempting to the novice and can confuse the logical with the illogical.

Before opening the envelope, the psychometrist should first indulge in some deep breathing before closing his or her eyes and meditating on the object he or she is handling. After recording the impressions received this way, the envelope may be opened and the actual piece of jewelry is handled until it submits all possible information. In a psychic workshop the students may pick up and read any envelope they choose and should attempt to read two or three pieces of jewelry at one meeting.

Psychometry is a rewarding method of predicting past, present and future events, but it is an exhausting exercise for the psychometrist. A short period of deep breathing and meditation can recharge the psychic batteries before the student attempts to move onto another exercise.

Touch and Tell

It is not necessary to use only jewelry for psychometry readings. Remember that the impressions you get from a piece of jewelry were transferred to that object because they had been worn and handled by the owner of the object. Therefore, direct contact with that person, such as holding hands, should yield even more powerful impressions. So, where possible, it is a good idea to start with the object and advance to using personal contact.

Missing People

Even a novice can help to locate a missing person by using basic psychometry. Other personal items such as clothing or a lock of hair can yield significant clues to the missing person's whereabouts. Some fragment of information which seems insignificant at the time can turn out to be an important piece of the jigsaw. Family and friends of missing people will often approach psychics to help in the search.

Crime

Because psychometry involves the sense of touch, the psychometrist can receive important impressions from any number of objects relating to a crime. Imagine a grieving relative of the person who has uncharacteristically committed suicide. The relative is unsure whether there was any foul play involved because there are no obvious signs of it. An instinct compels him or her to investigate the circumstances to find the truth, otherwise he or she is left in a state of limbo with no answer and therefore no closure.

By examining some of the deceased's personal belongings, the psychometrist might gather enough information to explain if and why such drastic action was taken, or if there was any foul play involved. Tell-tale signs, such as feelings and impressions of the person at the time of the crime will be left on his or her personal belongings.

In some psychic workshops, the teacher will collect pictures from newspapers of wanted criminals. The students hold one of the photos and report on the impressions they are receiving. Recorded for future reference when the crime is solved, it is amazing how accurate these impressions can be.

Lovers

Information about the future prospects of a love match is the most popular prediction sought by most people, including the members of a psychic workshop. For this exercise, you need an object that is a personal possession of your partner or your potential lover, preferably one that has had no previous owners. You place the object in an envelope before entering the workshop and place it in a basket. The basket is passed around the circle and each student randomly selects one item for examination.

The Importance Of Guardian Angels

MYSTERY AND MYTH SURROUND THE BELIEF THAT EACH OF US HAS AT LEAST
ONE SPIRIT GUIDE OR GUARDIAN ANGEL WHO IS ASSIGNED TO HELP US ON
OUR JOURNEY THROUGH LIFE.

What Are Guardian Angels and Spirit Guides

The choice of title — spirit guide or guardian angel — is personal. Spirit beings who guard over us must surely be angels, so I prefer to call my own spirit guide "guardian angel".

For hundreds of years it was thought by many people that the use of a Ouija board was the simplest and fastest way to communicate with their spirit guides. However, the entities that you contact through these means, regardless of their claims, are never your deceased relative, or your guardian angel or spirit guide. Instead, they are disembodied entities from the nether regions of the spirit world, and no matter how accurate they sometimes appear to be, they can be malicious and ultimately dangerous.

Communication with your guardian angel will not eventuate if your pursuit of psychic development is for the wrong reasons or you don't treat it with respect. If you want to develop a mutual understanding with your guardian angel, you will need to commit to the process of serious psychic development. Your guardian angel looks after your well-being, so pay it the respect it deserves by frequently thinking of it with love and thanking it whenever it assists you.

If you allow your communication skills to become more finely tuned, you will discover there are many instances when your guardian angel intervenes on your behalf to bring about a favorable outcome regarding romantic, business or health issues. We tend to keep our guardian angels very much on their spiritual toes with our petty grievances. However, it seems that because of recent New Age thinking, guardian angels are more acknowledged and appreciated than at any other time.

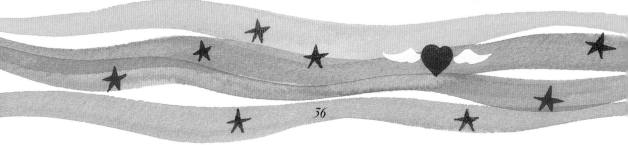

The Role of a Guardian Angel

The main role of your guardian angel is to assist you in your spiritual evolvement and protect you from danger, if that is appropriate, or at the least warn you of it — you, however, need to listen to those warnings that usually come in the form of a strong intuitive feeling. People occasionally report that their survival of a near-fatal accident was accompanied by a glimpse of their guardian angels. An interesting example that I've heard about involved a woman who fell off a cliff. She suddenly felt herself being swept up in someone's arms as a gust of air blew her onto the ledge below.

Guardian angels are highly evolved spirits who understand that while you are living on a material planet, you will need to learn material values as much as spiritual values. They are here to help you balance the material with the spiritual. They respect the fact that you have a free will to make important decisions and choices, and though they may tug at your conscience when you flirt with danger, they understand that you must learn through experience. Guardian angels have no desire to intrude upon your privacy. It is not the role of guardian angels to judge your lifestyle nor is it their job to decide your beliefs.

The more you respect your guardian angel, the more it will help you.

Your guardian angel will enlist the help of other specialist angels or "devas" (the Indian word for angels that is now commonly used in the West). These angels were created as angels, while many guardian angels were once human beings. The angels or devas specialize in healing or in helping people or plants grow. There is an angel for everything that requires its help. Guardians angels ask the specialist angels to help them in their tasks. The hierarchy of angels is: the Archangel Raphael, then the angels or devas, followed by the guardian angels.

The term "guardian angel" may conjure up visual impressions of ethereal beings but, if and when you ever see yours, you may be surprised to discover how ordinary it looks. The important thing is to believe and trust in the work guardian angels do on your behalf. And remember, they are not simply invisible welfare workers.

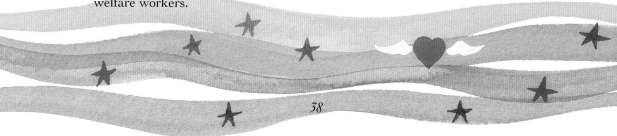

How to Recognize Your Guardian Angel

Guardian angels rarely make their presence known through ghostly apparitions. They can be quite creative and even comical in finding ways to get your attention. They may use a distinct signal as their calling card. For instance, if a buzzing sound always happens in your ears or in your head just before you receive a premonition, you will soon identify it with your guardian angel. Other signals may be a churning up feeling in the pit of your stomach; the hairs standing up on the back of your neck; a sudden gust of wind brushing against your face when there is no breeze; objects being removed from their usual place but safely turning up in the least likely place you would put them. These are a few of a guardian angel's calling cards.

Though very few people see apparitions, those who can should recognize the difference between their guardian angel and a haunting spirit. A chilled atmosphere accompanies haunting entities or poltergeists and you will feel frightened. A cool breeze will arrive with your guardian angel, and your guardian angels instills peace and comfort, even when it is trying to attract your attention.

Occasionally guardian angels try to attract your attention by doing things that could frighten you. For example, they might knock the telephone receiver off the hook a couple of times or switch the TV channel over or even turn the TV on and off. These comical little incidents only happen when you have forgotten to do something important and, unlike similar incidents caused by poltergeists, will stop as soon as you have remembered what you were supposed to do or where you were supposed to be at the time. Through personal signals such as these you will soon get to know when your guardian angel is around you, and this helps develop your communication and your relationship.

Building a Relationship with Your Guardian Angel

Once you have accepted the fact that you have a guardian angel, the next most important step is to find a way of direct communication with it so that you can build up a happy and satisfactory relationship. This friendship deserves the same respect and appreciation as any other kind of relationship. If you wish to attract a special someone into your life, you immediately try to find out that person's likes and dislikes, what interests him or her, his or her preferred environment, favorite color, and what sort of music he or she appreciates.

Good relationships prosper with good communication skills and are nourished by the quality time invested in them. You must ask yourself how much energy you are willing to contribute to this relationship. Naturally, it takes more time and effort to build up a relationship with someone who lives in a far-off land and speaks a different language. No one will assume it is easy to overcome these barriers, but anyone who has been willing to try can tell you it is worth it.

Creating or joining a psychic workshop will teach you the necessary skills to build a relationship with your guardian angel. Once you have established contact with your new friend it is a natural progression to break down any barriers that may restrict you from building a lasting and mutually satisfactory relationship.

Under psychic workshop conditions, the guardian angel of one of the students will occasionally make its presence felt or seen by other members of the group. This is a sign of approval from the spirit so it is a good idea to be prepared for these conditions. For example, each student should choose two questions for the guardian angel to answer. One question could be of a personal nature and the other should be about psychic development. All the information received about psychic development should be recorded at each meeting so that time is not wasted repeating the same questions.

On these occasions there is tremendous psychic power at work, and much progress is made.

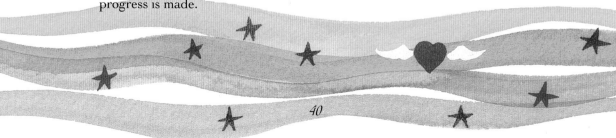

Distinguishing between Departed
Loved Ones and Your Guardian Angel

If you should see a deceased loved one, do not be quick to assume that this person is now your guardian angel. Your guardian angel may be a relative who died before you were born; however, its existence in your life is purely to look after your spiritual well-being. Your deceased loved one on the other hand will usually appear in order to reassure you that he or she is happy and well.

A friend of mine who is highly psychic, just as her mother was, and who has witnessed ghostly apparitions of deceased relatives and other spirit beings, including apparitions of her guardian angels, is married to a man who claims to have an open mind about psychic phenomena. My friend and her mother always suspected the husband was simply indulging their "fantasies" by listening to their accounts of these experiences.

When my friend's mother was very ill, her daughter and son-in-law visited her in hospital. While they were discussing the afterlife, my friend and her mother challenged the husband about his true beliefs, and he admitted that he had always been very skeptical about ghostly apparitions. His mother-in-law promised that after she died she would do her best to find a way to prove to him that psychic phenomena and ghostly apparitions were real. Some twelve months after his mother-in-law's death, he was driving his wife to work. As he glanced in his rearview mirror, he became unnerved, almost causing an accident, because there before his eyes sat his mother-in-law in the back seat of the car, smiling at him. He turned around to make sure he wasn't hallucinating and, as he later described the incident, the lady smiled at him, winked, and said, "I told you so".

WHEN TO USE YOUR PSYCHIC ABILITY

ONCE DEVELOPED, YOUR PSYCHIC ABILITY BECOMES SECOND NATURE. IT
WILL FLOW AS EASILY AS ANY OF YOUR OTHER FIVE SENSES, ALL OF WHICH
WILL NOW EXTEND INTO THE PSYCHIC REALM.

From the time you are recognized as a psychic, your life takes on a whole
new meaning. Psychics are as popular for their ability to predict the future,
as they are for their ability to contact the spirits of deceased loved ones. It
therefore becomes necessary for the psychic to take control of the demands
made on their time by people seeking their advice. Many people will seek
the benefit of your psychic skills, but most will not want you to stop —
something you must do, if you are to recharge your psychic batteries.

There are many important circumstances in which the use of your
psychic skills can bring great relief to people. Police departments all over
the world are no longer afraid to include the psychic's input in solving
crime, especially when it comes to locating missing people. As for yourself,
accidents might be avoided. Catastrophes caused by nature such as land
slides, hurricanes, fire and floods cannot be stopped, but you may able to
arrange to be absent from the scene if you heed the warnings of a psychic.
Health problems may also benefit from the power of psychic healing (see
Psychic Healing, pages 62–65).

Ghost Busting

There are some people who, when they die, have difficulty leaving the
material plane. It could be because the person died suddenly and is
resistant to accepting his or her death. While his or her guardian angel and
a deceased relative are there from the moment the person was in danger, the
person's resistance prevents him or her from seeing or hearing them. A
psychic can be of real assistance here. He or she will call on the guardian
angel and the spirits of the deceased relatives of the earth-bound soul. As
soon as this person is able to see his or her loved ones from the other side,
he or she is willing to leave and go with them into the light.

When You Should Not Use Your Psychic Ability

It is both unwise and irresponsible to predict misfortune for someone who will be a pre-destined victim of accident, crime, natural disaster or fatal disease. Sometimes, when you are using your psychic ability to predict the future for someone, you will have a distant impression of a terrible situation like the ones mentioned above and will wonder whether you should deliver the message.

It has always been my firm belief that only predictions that are positive or which can reverse an unhappy situation should be passed on. To begin with, no psychic, no matter how experienced, will claim 100 percent accuracy — so it is possible for you to misinterpret the prediction. As well as that, imagine how you would feel if a psychic told you that you were going to become the victim of a violent attack from which you could not escape, or that a drunken driver was going to run you down.

However, if you should be doing a psychic reading for someone who was going to get behind the wheel of a car while they were intoxicated, and you could see that person being responsible for an accident, then you must certainly tell them about the outcome of their behavior.

You should not use your psychic ability in any form if you are intoxicated or under the influence of drugs, or when you are experiencing emotional upheaval or depression. You should not use your psychic skills to predict the future for people who are likely to become dependent on you to solve all their problems — psychic ability is supposed to help people help themselves.

CAUTION

There are certain times and conditions that are unfavorable for practicing psychic development. We all experience negative emotions from time to time, such as depression, confusion, paranoia, and revenge. These are times when we cannot benefit from exerting the degree of energy it takes to pursue psychic development.

HOW TO CREATE A PSYCHIC ATMOSPHERE

CREATING THE RIGHT KIND OF POSITIVE ENERGY IS EXTREMELY IMPORTANT FOR YOUR SPECIAL PLACE OF PSYCHIC DEVELOPMENT. THE AMBIENCE NEEDS TO BE CALMING AND PEACEFUL.

Whatever environment you choose for the purpose of your psychic development, you should feel an intimacy with the vibration within its walls. While many people like the idea of conducting a psychic workshop out of doors, there are too many distractions of nature that will disturb your proceedings and which you would not want to interfere with anyway. When spiritual or religious ceremonies are conducted inside an enclosed space the energy is contained within that area, thus increasing its power.

Choosing the Place

The place you choose should be well ventilated so that the psychic energy can easily flow to all parts of the room. Its size should be comfortable so that intimacy can be maintained. Remember that the place you choose will become your psychic workshop, so availability is an important factor. For instance, if you choose one of the rooms in your house for this purpose, it should be a room that will not be entered by anyone other than those who will be attending the workshop, and it should be located as far from distracting noises as possible. If such a room is impossible to find in your home, maybe another member of your group has a suitable room in his or her house.

Before you start your workshop activities, it would be a good idea for the group to meet in your chosen environment a few times just to sit around relaxing, discussing psychic phenomena and spiritual subjects, and building up a psychic atmosphere. Try practicing short periods of meditation. Concentrate on your guardian angels. Invite them in — after all, they are going to become regular visitors to the workshop once you begin.

Cleansing Your New Psychic Workshop

Before you move into the house that is to become your new home, the first thing you do is to clean the place thoroughly before decorating it to suit the needs and personality of you and your family. Similarly, you need to cleanse the atmosphere in your new psychic workshop to clear any old or negative energies that will disturb the psychic power you and your group wish to create.

The cleansing process is important because positive psychic energy attracts powerful spirit contact and promotes psychic growth. Students of a newly cleansed psychic workshop will find it easier to direct their thoughts to psychic activities when there are no atmospheric distractions or disturbances.

Sometimes it is necessary to rent a venue for your workshop development that is used at other times for activities that create energies incompatible with your own. If the cleansing process is not done before your psychic workshop begins, these leftover energies can combine and conflict with your group's collective psychic energy. Thus direct spirit contact with the more highly evolved spirits you are seeking cannot be guaranteed.

The other reason for cleansing the atmosphere before a session with the psychic workshop is to remove any unfriendly, unsuited spirit visitors who will otherwise be attracted to your group. They can be as difficult to remove as a human being who invades a social gathering in order to cause trouble. This is a time when prevention is better than cure.

What You Will Need

All of the members of the psychic workshop should be present for the cleansing ceremony. Membership numbers should be restricted to a minimum of three and a maximum of twelve. For the purpose of this exercise we will assume that there are twelve members. To perform this ceremony, you will need a round table covered by a white tablecloth onto which are placed the following objects: twelve white candles, three essential oils (lemongrass, frankincense and myrrh), an essential-oil burner, a bowl of water, a small dish of table salt, and twelve pieces of paper with the words of a cleansing ceremony affirmation printed on them.

The Ceremony

The members of the workshop form a circle around the table and each takes one candle. The candles are now lit, as is the essential-oil burner. Each member takes a paper which holds the cleansing affirmation below. The group relaxes with a few moments of deep breathing, and then, as the members of the group turn first toward the North, they recite the words of the affirmation:

> *We evoke the collective psychic forces of*
> *the universe to attend the cleansing of*
> *this establishment and we dedicate this ceremony to*
> *the purpose of psychic development.*

The affirmation is repeated three more times as the group continues to turn toward the East, South and West. One of the members then proceeds to sprinkle the water in each corner of the room, while another member follows, sprinkling the salt around the floor as they go. The ceremony is then completed.

Cleansing Your Aura

Just as the physical body requires constant cleansing, so too does the aura require a cleansing process. The aura is the energy field of rainbow-like colors around the body. Cleansing it keeps it strong so that you can resist negative attitudes and psychic leaches. Psychics who can see auras will use words like luminous, vibrant, colorful, bright, dull, heavy, limp, dark and murky to describe the conditions they see.

Negative energy in the atmosphere can temporarily damage the aura. Other people can feed on your aura when their own is damaged, and be totally unaware that they are doing it. Physical disorders appear in the aura before the condition manifests within the physical body.

It is interesting to note that people with the psychic ability to see auras are not only able to interpret the physical and emotional condition of a person, but also the level of their spiritual evolvement. The degree of well-being of both the physical and the spiritual is determined by the vibrancy of the colors in the aura. These colors represent specific aspects of a person. Colors which suggest a person is highly evolved spiritually are vivid gold and/or bright white. Vivid blue or green signifies good physical health conditions. Murky gray or black reveals poor health, poor self-esteem, and a lack of faith in spiritual matters or human nature.

How to Cleanse Your Aura

Now that you understand the importance of cleansing the aura, you need to learn how to visualize its locality and practice the following simple exercises of the cleansing ceremony. You will need a full-length mirror, a small table onto which you place a white candle, an essential-oil burner and some lemongrass essential oil, a small dish of water, and a card or paper containing the aura-cleansing affirmation.

Begin burning the lemongrass oil and light the candle. Stand in front of the mirror about one foot (30 cm) away from it. Take a deep breath by inhaling deeply and then holding your breath for a few seconds; exhale slowly. Repeat five times.

Now look into the mirror and focus your attention at a point somewhere in the middle of your chest. Let your eyes drift to a point about six inches (15 cm) above your head. Do not stare. Imagine you are basking in the sunlight, eyes almost half-closed, then let your eyes follow this arc all the way around your body.

As you continue to glance around the outside of your body in this semi-trance state, try to meditate and visualize this energy field as you chant the words of this affirmation:

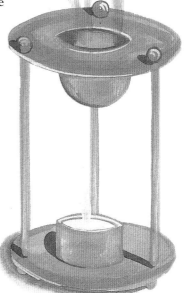

This is my aura, it belongs to me
It is a vital part of my being.
I evoke my intuitive power to
Open my mind and my eyes to the
Beauty of the color and the light within.
So mote it be.

Repeat the affirmation for as long as the exercise takes to complete. The first time you are successful in seeing the aura, the excitement you feel may disturb the serenity of the atmosphere you have created and you lose the picture. This is a natural occurrence, so don't be alarmed or disappointed. The next time you will be ready for it.

To close the cleansing ceremony, sprinkle the water over your aura and end by putting an imaginary white light of protection around you.

Creating a Joyous Atmosphere

Whatever the occasion may be, it is only natural that we try to create an appropriate atmosphere. Weddings conjure up a joyous atmosphere that is enhanced by pretty flowers, satin and lace, and background music playing romantic melodies. The guests adorn themselves with brightly colored clothing, and the atmosphere is alive with the aroma of many perfumes.

Creating a psychic environment deserves the same attention to detail as any other important event. In this case you are going to create a joyous atmosphere for yourself and your guardian angels. Ambient music that emits the sounds of nature will relax and loosen the mind. Fabrics in psychic colors, such as soft-toned blues, greens and lilacs should be worn by members of the group and can be draped around the psychic workshop area. The ethereal glow of white candles creates a psychic-enhancing atmosphere, as does the aroma of essential oils, such as lavender which soothes the heart and mind. For further psychic power, add crystals such as amethyst which induces a state of tranquillity, yellow fluorite to help give a sense of inner peace while enhancing mental clarity, and tiger's eye for balancing the emotions and awakening the intuition.

By creating such good vibrations, you are encouraging and inviting your guardian angels into a welcoming atmosphere. Positive energy encourages the development of your psychic awareness and evokes highly evolved spirits who can more easily communicate under these conditions. Furthermore, if you make your guardian angels happy, they are more inclined to help you with special favors. For instance, you may wish to contact the spirit of a deceased loved one. People on the other side do not become advanced psychic beings overnight. They also need to develop certain skills if you are to communicate with them. Your guardian angel can teach your loved one how to communicate with you.

Creating a joyous atmosphere for your psychic workshop also puts all the members of the group on the same wavelength. This builds up a communicative energy, making progress easier and more enjoyable.

Some psychic circles will even nominate a special day of the year that is dedicated to their guardian angels, naming it "Guardian Angels' Day". On this occasion they observe the celebration by creating a suitable atmosphere, as previously described, and chanting specially dedicated verses, which the members create themselves, such as:

Joyously and lovingly I celebrate this day
In honor of my guardian angel who shows me the way
Of light and life, of truth and love, of happiness and giving,
To share with someone else the harmony of living.

They then fulfill this promise by deliberately performing a good deed for someone in need, in gratitude for the many times that their guardian angels have helped them.

Psychic Shields

Some people are so eager to develop their psychic ability that it never occurs to them that there are almost as many negative forces waiting to invade a psychic circle as there are positive ones, and so they leave themselves open to the dangers of entering the realms of the unknown without protection.

It is worth noting that while you may be very happy to contact the spirits of deceased loved ones, such power also attracts uninvited guests who may be harmless, but who don't want to leave. This is why the opening and closing ceremonies discussed on pages 58–61 are so important.

The Essential White Light

Everyone in a psychic circle should visualize a circle of light around themselves and every other person and object in the room, as well as the area where psychic power is to be used. Imagine the white light as a brilliant halo symbolizing purity and good intention, which is to be used as a protective shield as you chant the words to this affirmation:

May this pure circle of white light envelop me
These objects and this environment
So that no harm or ill intent may enter its vicinity.
I ask this protection for the sincere purpose
Of psychic development.
So mote it be.

You may wish to use this method of protection in other circumstances, such as before you set off on a journey — in this case, place the light around yourself and then around the vehicle — or to help the healing process of a loved one who is sick and quell any fears of someone about to go into surgery. You can also put a circle of white light around children while they are out of your care.

Just as you would not enter unknown territory without a survival kit, you should not explore the spirit world without your psychic shields.

Talismans and Amulets

Talismans and amulets come in all shapes and sizes. They can be purchased at any shop that sells New Age merchandise for the use of protection. Two talismans used for protection in psychic circles are drawings or figurines of the lotus and the moon. Drawings of the five-pointed star or pentacle are a familiar wall-hanging in psychic circles because legend has it that this symbol has enormous power.

Crystals, such as the ones mentioned in this chapter, project energies that repel evil influences, and can be carried on your person, placed in appropriate positions, or put under your pillow. Coral beads are reputed to ward off bad luck. The Crucifix is one of many religious talismans worn for spiritual inspiration and protection from evil. Apart from the popular belief that good luck is attracted by a horseshoe talisman, there is a further belief that wherever the horseshoe hangs, the Devil will not enter and you will often find a horseshoe hanging on the wall of a room where psychic meetings are held.

Talismans for Attracting Love and Happiness

A black cat talisman is one of the most favorite of symbols for good luck. Beads of stone and crystal are also widely used as talismans. Crystal beads are a popular choice for attracting good luck in love and finance. The old superstition that a necklace of amber beads will ensure the faithfulness of a partner and produce healthy children is particularly believed by people from Middle and Eastern European backgrounds. Coral beads, apart from warding off bad luck, are also reputed to improve health problems, and beads of jet inspire courage.

When the Crucifix is enclosed by a circle it symbolizes the preservation of life and eternity. Long life and domestic bliss are signified by a dragon-shaped talisman. Heart-shaped lockets containing a lock of hair or photograph of a deceased relative are sometimes placed in the circle of a psychic workshop to encourage the spirit of that person to make contact.

Psychic Circles

Any fears, phobias or misconceptions you may have before you begin your workshop activities will be dispelled by your teacher. And you should not be afraid to inform your teacher of any last minute jitters — it is his or her job to reassure you that he or she can teach you how to harness your psychic ability.

If you have no idea where to begin to look for your nearest psychic workshop, you will find this information in newspapers devoted to psychic subjects or by telephoning a psychic center listed in your local telephone directory. Spiritual church meetings are advertised in local newspapers, and any of the members will know where and when your nearest psychic workshop is held. Often a small donation is requested from you, and sometimes a fee is necessary, but these are usually only expected by advanced workshops, run by professional psychics who contribute much time and effort to the development of their students.

The ideal number of students in a psychic workshop is between six and 12. Psychic workshops are usually held at night because the atmosphere is calmer at this time. Most people are afraid of psychic activity after dark because this is the time ghosts and spirits are said to be seen. Ghosts and spirits are in fact more likely to be encountered at night, the reason being that the conditions of the atmosphere are not so dense with other activity and it's easier to communicate with them.

Though it is preferable to conduct psychic workshops at night, the most important consideration for the scheduling of workshop times should be the convenience of its students.

A Meditation Technique

There are many meditation techniques available. If you belong to a psychic workshop, the group will have its own method. The method described below may suit you, but first find a quiet space where you will not be disturbed. Either lie down or sit comfortably with your back straight. Let your hands rest with your palms open.

When you are comfortable, focus on your feet and relax them. Do the same as you move your focus up through your body to your ankles, calves, knees, thighs, buttocks, back, chest, shoulders, arms, hands, neck, scalp and face.

Turn your attention to your breath. Feel the air move into your nose and fill your lungs. Be aware of how the air causes your chest to rise; then feel your chest contract as the air leaves your lungs, exiting your body through your mouth or nose. Be careful not to alter your normal pattern of breathing, just quietly observe it. Increase your focus by counting the breaths. Count one beat for the inhalation and one beat for each exhalation — in *one*, out *one*; in *two*, out *two*; in *three*, out *three*, and so on.

As thoughts move into your mind, do not attempt to get rid of them. Instead, be an observer of your thoughts without judgment. Then return your focus to your breath and your observation of how each breath feels in your body.

Developing Your Psychic Ability On Your Own

Developing your psychic ability does not necessitate your joining a psychic circle. You may prefer to work alone. In this case, choose your favorite room and follow the procedures and exercises described within this book.

The Importance of Student Compatibility

Compatibility between the students and their teachers can make the difference between rapid or slow psychic development for the whole group. A good teacher will have discretely engineered a situation where he or she was able to examine your interaction with the other students. Sometimes, however, a purely self-serving student will slip through, and it takes only one person's insincerity to disrupt the flow of the good psychic energy the teamwork of a compatible psychic group can generate.

Trust

Many guarded family secrets are inadvertently brought to light during psychic meetings with guardian angels and the spirits of deceased relatives. I can recall a particularly sensitive example of this situation when a young woman tried to contact the spirit of her deceased father who supposedly died when she was three years old, and who was born, raised and died in England. This young woman had been raised in an orphanage with antiquated rules, so her family history was sketchy.

We were all surprised to learn from the spirit of a deceased American that he was her father. It seems she was the result of an adulterous affair between himself and her mother, also deceased. He went on to explain that he had wanted to rear his daughter but was encouraged to leave the country. As a result of this she was left with the mother and her stepfather who both abandoned her. He told her that the man she called "Father" was still alive and living in England. It was a most traumatic but enlightening story, which, by the way, all proved to be true. This kind of shared information builds up a trustful bond between the group.

Avoiding Negative Thinkers

It is not uncommon for people experiencing an emotionally disturbed period in their lives to become negative in their thoughts, words and deeds. When this kind of energy is brought into a psychic circle it is a natural deterrent to good psychic power, and can even attract unwelcome spirits into the circle. Like attracts like, and just as the person in emotional trauma becomes dependent on the positive energy of the other members of the group, so too do the disturbed spirits they attract.

This is not to say that everyone should desert a fellow member who is suffering. On the contrary, you are in a powerful position to help this person reverse their negative period if he or she is prepared to listen and trust you to act in his or her best interests. If this help is refused, you must encourage your troubled friend to take time out from his or her psychic development until he or she is able to put his or her priorities in order.

As for the unwelcome spirit visitors who are much more difficult to persuade to leave, you could try the circle of white light and some affirmations or other psychic shields to combat the negativity they create.

When your psychic ability is well developed, you can also detect a negative person's vibration in everyday life. Under these conditions, if you cannot avoid the person, the fastest and easiest method is to visualize the circle of white light being placed around you so that the negative energy emitted by their aura cannot penetrate your own aura.

This is also a good method of protection against an attack by a vicious animal. Not only will it protect you by discouraging the animal, the power of the white light will soothe the animal's fear or anger.

Opening and Closing the Psychic Circle

Psychic workshop meetings usually take about two hours — the first hour is devoted to opening up the circle, meditation and two or three psychic exercises that open and develop the senses. The second hour is devoted to the happy hour and closing the circle.

The Opening

For this very special ceremony that immediately follows the cleansing ceremony, all the members of the psychic workshop should be present. A table is placed in the center of a circle of chairs — one chair for each member of the group. On the table are placed psychic-enhancing objects. Among these are two white candles and an essential-oil burner, which are immediately lit. The type of essential oil is a matter of collective choice. A small selection of crystals is often placed around the table, as well as two pamphlets containing the words to the affirmations for the opening and closing ceremonies.

Before being seated the group stands around the table. Turning Northward they begin to chant the affirmation which opens up the circle. This is repeated three more times as the members turn toward the East, South and West.

> *In the name of this psychic circle, and in the*
> *best interests of the development of psychic power,*
> *we invoke the divine intervention of our guardian*
> *angels to guide us in our psychic workshop activities.*
> *We ask this in good faith and in the belief that our*
> *achievement will benefit the universe.*
> *So mote it be.*

The group continues to stand, holding hands to form a complete circle. A few minutes of deep breathing exercises follow, then the members are seated. When comfortable, they begin a period of meditation, concentrating on their intuitive powers and visualizing the psychic energy which is now emitted and enveloping the circle. They continue by visualizing the presence of their individual guardian angels, silently welcoming them into the circle. This process takes about fifteen minutes.

The teacher then directs the members of the group to open their eyes and slowly relax each muscle of the body and mind. The teacher will then suggest that they now think only peaceful, positive thoughts for the duration of the workshop meeting.

Exercises

It is customary that the first exercise of every psychic workshop is an elementary test of its basic psychometry skills. Each member is offered an empty envelope into which they place a piece of personal jewelry. Naturally, the other members must not see who placed what in which envelope. The envelopes are then placed in a basket, mixed up, and are passed out at random to each member.

No one is expected to produce infallible predictions from the handling of the concealed objects — at least not at this early stage.

Another customary practice at psychic workshops is for someone (usually the teacher) to take notes of the predictions made by the psychometry readings. These notes become part of the workshop's logbook to be referred to later for a progress report. While handling the envelopes, the students are encouraged to share any information or impressions they receive with the rest of the group, no matter how insignificant the impressions seem to be. There are usually exclamations of surprise at this point as the students slowly identify their jewelry by association with the predictions being made.

This exercise is then followed by another period of deep breathing and meditation during which they are encouraged to focus on the spirit of a deceased loved one. Miracles don't happen immediately, but there is seldom a workshop that goes by without some significant psychic activity. A mixture of apprehension and excitement at these encounters usually takes up what time is left of the meeting.

The Closing

Closing down the circle is an important part of the psychic workshop's activities. It must be remembered that no one likes to be on call 24 hours a day, but if you don't close down the circle appropriately, it will be like leaving the communication lines permanently open between the group and its guardian angels and other spirit entities.

Guardian angels do not relate to our concept of time, so they don't always know when we need them to vacate our space for short periods of time to allow us to go about the business of living on our material planet. A respect for their role in our lives and their respect for our concept of time is not an impossible task to achieve with the help of good communication skills.

Once you have built up a good relationship with your guardian angel, it will not mind being on call for arranged times of psychic workshop activities, nor will it reject your sincere request for it to leave the premises when the workshop is closed.

To close the circle, extinguish candles and the essential-oil burner, and place a white velvet cloth over the psychic shields. Students join hands in a silent meditation for a few minutes while they visualize the exit of guardian angels and other spirit entities. Then, facing North, they chant the words of the closing down affirmation, repeating the verse as they continue to face East, South and West.

We wish to thank our guardian angels and other
spirit friends for their kind attendance
to our psychic workshop. We appreciate the help
we have received and promise to endeavor to
continue to develop our psychic potential.
It is now time to say goodbye — so we wish
you well, but we wish you to return to your
own spiritual realms until we meet again.
So mote it be.

The circle is now closed, and you will leave with plenty to think about, yet free to continue your normal activities.

While your guardian angel likes to exchange intimate time with you, you
should be careful not to be always asking it to fix every little problem in your
life. You are supposed to make the effort to try and work out your
problems for yourself, however, your guardian angel will be
happy to help you help yourself.

Psychic Healing

Even in this time of New Age thinking, alternative medicine and psychic awareness, spiritual or psychic healing is often considered by many people as a last resort when all else fails. Yet various methods of psychic healing have been practiced since the earliest times. People have never lost their fascination with this form of healing, and while many people who practice it are genuine, there are many who are not. And it is not uncommon for an ordinary individual to have a profound healing effect on an upset or physically ill person, just by touching them, stroking them or through massage. Some modern doctors seem to have an uncanny ability to diagnose illness as well as an apparent ability to transfer vital energy to patients.

All forms of psychic healing involve the transference of vital energies from one source or another. The vital energy can be drawn from the atmosphere, from nature, from the healer or from other people. Many psychic healers believe they are mediums for special healing angels or their own guardian angel.

The most common methods of psychic healing are vital magnetic healing, clairvoyance, psychometry and telepathy. Faith healing has never lost its popularity — individuals will meditate on their vision of the universal being alone or in a group, with or without the help of an experienced healer.

Faith Healing

Each year since Bernadette Soubsirous' vision of the Virgin Mary at Lourdes in 1858, thousands of pilgrims have visited the shrine to bathe in its waters, believing and praying for some divine intervention. Many claim miracle cures, and even though very few of these cures are certified as miracles, the faithful are undeterred and will return whenever they can. Faith healing was common among early Christians since the time that Jesus and then his apostles tended to the sick.

Vital Magnetic Energy

When a healer is using vital magnetic energy, he or she is drawing vital energy from the atmosphere, from nature or from spiritual sources, which is then transferred to the patient by the healer's hands. Its purpose is to relieve congestion of fluids in the body and to increase the flow of nervous energy to relax and revive the patient. When massage is performed by someone with sensitive hands, the results will be very impressive. The healer's right and left hands act as poles for the discharge of energy. When healers pass their hands over their patients, they are directing this energy to relieve congested areas and to feed depleted areas.

The practice known as "laying on of hands" makes use of vital magnetic energy. It is an ancient form of healing and has never lost its popularity. Between the eleventh and nineteenth centuries, it was a common belief in Europe that kings and queens had the power to heal the sick by the laying on of hands, a process known during this period as the Royal Touch. Valentine Greatrakes, born in 1629 and generally referred to as the "Irish Stroker" because he healed through stroking the ill, was a commoner who at the age of 33 claimed that he also possessed the gift of the Royal Touch. Even though his claims gave rise to resentment from the royal courts, he was allowed to practice his skills.

A century later Franz Anton Mesmer's theory of animal magnetism created enthusiasm throughout Europe. After earning a medical degree in 1766 Mesmer began to formulate his theory of an invisible flow of magnetic current through all objects in the universe, including the human body. Mesmer claimed that health was dependent on harmony between the energy within and outside the body — this ensures the alignment of an individual life-force with the universal.

Absent Healing by Telepathy

For healing by telepathy to work, it is necessary that the minds of the healer and the patient be in harmony. When a healer directs concentrated thought to the person in need of assistance, that person will react with a feeling of hope, which in turn revitalizes that person who can then access his or her own body's healing mechanisms.

The results of absent healing may be even stronger if the receiver is unaware that the healer is sending him or her healing energy. When the patient is aware of the healer's attempts, he or she could become anxious for results or try too hard to be responsive and thus set up mental barriers.

Healing by Psychometry

Because the skills of psychometrists lie in their heightened sense of touch, all they need do to diagnose the cause of a physical problem is touch the patient, usually by holding his or her hand, or hold some object the patient has handled. Through this touching, the psychic makes contact with the patient's physical and etheric bodies. Any imbalances will be felt by the psychometrist who will then attempt to diagnose them.

Healing by Clairvoyance

A clairvoyant does not touch the patient, but will often run his or her hands above the patient to sense where congestion or inflammation is occurring, then they will use their intuition to interpret what they find. Clairvoyants usually work with a healing angel or their own guardian angel.

Charlatans

When people become desperate for help in curing their serious health problems, and can find no satisfactory answers through orthodox medicine, they may become afraid, vulnerable and gullible enough to trust anyone who claims to be able to cure them. Unfortunately, there are many charlatans just waiting to take advantage of such a person's weakened situation. Medical investigators have had little trouble in exposing some of the most ruthless of these charlatans.

Many genuine psychic healers suffer from the ridicule these exposures create. It takes a great deal of courage to overcome such criticism, and the efforts of a genuine healer can be weakened by the constant demand for proof of their skills. However, it is always necessary to visit your doctor after a session with a psychic healer to verify the effectiveness of the psychic healing.

The famous Brazilian healer Arigó, who died in 1971, was at first regarded as a charlatan and was closely scrutinized. But investigators were baffled by his ability to perform psychic surgery with little more than a pocket-knife and prescription medicine, without anesthesia or antiseptics. After successfully treating a politician suffering from an inoperable lung tumor he received respect and recognition. When Arigó was asked how he arrived at a diagnosis, he answered: "I simply listen to a voice in my right ear, and I repeat exactly what I hear — it is always right."

There are many good and sincere psychic healers, who, like Arigó, believe that they are just a vessel through which a spirit healer is working. In a psychic workshop, many stories such as this one about the healing career of Arigó are discussed, because they offer inspiration and encouragement to the student of psychic healing.

Healing in the Psychic Workshop

For the purpose of developing psychic ability in a modern psychic workshop, students are introduced to the healing process through meditation, where they are encouraged to focus on their own abilities to heal and diagnose sickness.

Each student takes a turn at moving his or her hands over and around the aura of another student who acts as the patient by lying on the floor and relaxing the body. The students are then asked to distinguish any differences they notice while they are feeling the energy generated from the aura. For example: "Is there an area which is colder or hotter than the rest of the patient's aura?" "Do you feel energized or have you been drained of energy?"

Once these differences are detected, the student is encouraged by his or her discovery. The students are reminded that at this stage they are merely observers of a medical condition. They are not qualified to accurately diagnose or heal the illness.

Happy Hour

You have been working hard during the first hour of the psychic workshop and now you want to relax and try out your favorite exercise without any pressure or rules. The idea is that you have fun and entertain each other. You drink cups of tea and then read the leaves. Someone will take the crystal ball from the table, and others will try out their newest skills in psychometry, the Tarot and playing card reading. The group then discusses any psychic experiences that anyone has had outside the psychic circle. Following this, the group divides into pairs of their own choosing to practice their skills. This is how each person discovers what will later become his or her specialty.

Telepathy

Once the students have chosen their partners, each pair is seated opposite each other with a divider between them. A curtain will suffice for this exercise. One person is selected to transmit a symbol or message and the other becomes the receiver. Each person is allowed three attempts at transmitting, then the roles are reversed. All results are recorded, and if they wish to, the students are allowed to change partners. This way you discover who are the transmitters and who are the receivers in your psychic circle. The three symbols selected for transmitting should be as diverse as possible, for instance, a specific animal, a date on the calendar, a celebrity.

Tarot Readings

A student chooses the person in the group he or she knows least about to demonstrate a Tarot card reading, and the two students decide who will be the reader and who will be the client. The client is invited to mix the cards face down on the table, put them back into a pack and shuffle the pack, while he or she concentrates on a question he or she wishes to ask. The cards are then handed back to the reader who proceeds to cut the cards into three piles, turns them face up, and then tries to interpret what the client's question was as well as the answer.

Guardian Angel Contact

For this demonstration the students sit in a comfortable position forming a circle. Deep breathing exercises and a short period of meditation follows, during which time all the members of the circle concentrate on making contact with their guardian angels. As soon as anyone makes contact, the group welcomes the spirit visitor and asks for a prediction for someone in the group. Sometimes only a few students will make contact, but rarely will there be "no contact made" recorded.

It is during this period that the spirits of deceased relatives often make contact with their surviving loved ones. Rarely do these spirits indulge in idle chatter, they usually are eager to make known some useful information for the contact or other relative, for instance, the spirit of the deceased father of a troubled teenager who is flirting with danger may be able to offer some individual advice for future reference, or a spirit may be able to enlighten the contact as to the whereabouts of a missing person or object. Whatever the message, you may be sure it will prove to be useful.

Affirmations

Chanting positive affirmations is a vital part of the happy hour in a psychic workshop. Affirmations are designed to reinforce a person's faith in his- or herself, his or her guardian angel, the psychic forces of the universe and the power of positive thought, word and deed. Affirmations chanted during the happy hour should be short declarations of your belief in the universal benefit of psychic development.

I believe in the truth and the light which
guides my psychic development.
I believe in my guardian angels
and in the sincerity of all my spirit contacts.
I believe that my intuition will
guide me toward a greater understanding
of myself and others.

Affirmations like these are easy for the student to remember, and the students will be encouraged to make contributions of their own creative verses.

MORNING

As I greet the dawning of this new day
I invoke the spirit of my Guardian Angel
to guide my actions, as I endeavor
to move one step forward in my
search for psychic awareness.

Today I will endeavor to contribute
to the psychic forces of the universe
by taking every opportunity that this
day brings to increase my psychic power,
which I will then transmit to the atmosphere
for the benefit of others. This is my pledge.
So mote it be.

NIGHT

As this day draws to its close,
I invoke the spirit of my Guardian Angel
to watch over me while I rest my physical body
and free my mind of all negative thought.
So mote it be.

Before I lie down to rest this night
I wish to thank the psychic forces of
the universe and my Guardian Angel for
the protection and guidance I have received this day.
So mote it be.

DISCOVERING YOUR SPECIALTY

GRADUALLY YOUR PSYCHIC DEVELOPMENT WILL EVOLVE TO A LEVEL WHERE YOU START TO FAVOR ONE METHOD OF PSYCHIC CRAFT OVER ALL THE OTHERS YOU HAVE LEARNED, MUCH LIKE A PERSON WHO GOES TO UNIVERSITY TO ACHIEVE A BACHELOR OF BUSINESS DEGREE, THEN GOES ON TO PRACTICE ACCOUNTANCY, OR A DOCTOR WHO STUDIES MEDICINE AND GOES ON TO SPECIALIZE IN PEDIATRICS.

Clairvoyance

Being clairvoyant means you have a supernatural power to visualize your predictions with clarity. If clairvoyance becomes your specialty you will need to acquire a descriptive vocabulary in order to relate your visual experiences in a manner that can be believed and understood by your client.

You should only report exactly what you see, do not presume to fill in the blanks of a sketchy visual experience. When you attempt to do so, you may be changing the whole concept of the message behind the pictures you are seeing. You are just a messenger who is given information on a strictly "need to know" basis. And even though the sketchy pictures you see make no sense at all to you personally, they will make perfect sense to your client. This person has the other pieces of the jigsaw.

Psychics and Morality

You should never make judgments when you do psychic readings for someone whose actions are regarded by you or society as inappropriate. Instead you suggest to the person that he or she tries to view his or her behavior as though it were the behavior of someone else and ask him- or herself whether this is how he or she wishes to be behaving. If so, ask your client if he or she understands the ramifications of such behavior and is he or she prepared to pay the price.

Psychic readings are highly confidential and nothing should induce you to divulge the confidential information with which you have been entrusted.

Clairaudience

Being a clairaudient means that you have the supernatural power to hear words, sentences or names transmitted from the spirit world.

Sometimes the words are loud and clear, but often they are muffled sounds that take intense concentration and patience to interpret. The supposed reason for this diversity is that the spirit who is attempting to catch your attention is not fully acquainted with this system of psychic communication.

Many clairaudients are unjustly branded fraudulent for their repeated attempts to sound out loudly, exactly what they are hearing. Often a clairaudient asks the client a question such as: "Do you know someone whose name begins with a *ju* or a *chu*?" Most people believe that the psychic is guessing and looking to them for more information. If you decide clairaudience is going to be your specialty, then you will have to suffer this kind of criticism. You will have no choice but to keep trying until the name or words become clearer or your client can identify the name with the scanty message attached. You must remember that your client cannot hear anything and your sometimes frail attempts to hear the words can be confusing to those who do not realize what's happening.

With time and practice you will have less difficulty understanding the messages that are being transmitted to you. Once you have reached this stage of development your client will understand more clearly his or her deceased loved one's message.

Despite the trials and tribulations a clairaudient has to go through, a good practitioner will ignore criticisms in favor of the challenge presented by this method of psychic activity.

Psychometry

If you would like the art of psychometry to become your specialty, then you need to understand how much can be involved in this method of predicting past, present and future events.

A skilled psychometrist is not expected to be restricted to reading items of jewelry or objects of that nature in order to predict the client's destiny. Personal contact through the psychometrist with the person or place concerned will render the same accurate results.

Psychometry for Health

Because psychometry involves prediction through the sense of touch, health problems can be revealed when the psychometrist gently runs his or her hands over the client's body. Physical disorders are often detected this way by a good psychometrist.

Crime

In some countries, the police will allow a psychometrist to examine the belongings of a criminal to gather information related to the crime. Such information may not be considered in a court of law, but can lead the authorities to evidence.

Romance

The most common reason people use the services of a psychometrist is to discover what they can about their love lives. They will gladly offer any photograph or personal object belonging to themselves or the person who is their current love interest in an effort to bring about a successful love connection. Naturally the more access the psychometrist has to the personal belongings of both parties, the more predictions he or she can offer the client, and the psychometrist's work is made easier. This does not mean that the psychometrist can make the other person feel or do anything he or she doesn't want to do, but the psychic can let the client know what the partner expects to give and take from the relationship. This enables the client to make an informed choice about his or her future love prospects.

Playing Cards

An ordinary deck of playing cards can be of good use in developing your psychic ability because you can use your intuitive skills to interpret the various combinations and layouts. You can be as creative as you wish in finding new ways to interpret time and events.

Perhaps because both the psychic and the client can view the Tarot cards or playing cards together, this method of predicting past, present and future events maintains its popularity. The client needs the skill of the psychic to interpret the meanings of various combinations, but seems to enjoy being part of the action by handling the cards and observing the psychic at work.

If you decide that this method of psychic prediction or fortune telling could be your specialty, you will discover that you never stop learning new and exciting meanings which the cards reveal, no matter how long you have been practicing the art of Tarot card reading.

The work you have done in the psychic workshop will prove to be invaluable to this fascinating skill. You will be free of the barriers that prevent a less psychically developed person from extending his or her mind to reach out and grasp the more subtle messages hidden within the symbols printed on the cards.

Due to its immense popularity, card reading can make you a slave to the craft if you do not take control of the demands made on your time for its services. Even when there is a fee attached, people still flock to card readers. Occasionally a client will declare that he or she doesn't really believe in it, but would "try it out — just for a laugh." Even when the client puts up this sort of barrier, a good card reader will soon convince him or her of its potency with an accurate reading.

The Meaning Of The Suits

THE SUIT OF HEARTS represent emotional issues: love and romance and family ties. The positive and negative influences that affect these aspects of life are examined by this suit. Hearts also represent the water signs, Cancer, Scorpio and Pisces.

THE SUIT OF CLUBS represent communication, energy, environment, and the positive and negative influences affecting these aspects of life. Clubs also represent the fire signs, Aries, Leo and Sagittarius.

THE SUIT OF DIAMONDS represent the material world, e.g. money, business, and the positive and negative influences affecting these aspects of life. Diamonds also represent the earth signs, Taurus, Virgo and Capricorn.

THE SUIT OF SPADES represent health both mental and physical, also the difficulties we must learn to deal with in life. Spades represent the air signs, Aquarius, Gemini and Libra.

Groups of Same Value in a Layout

ACES: 4 total success — 3 business negotiations — 2 marriage
KINGS: 4 reward for effort — 3 promotion — 2 minor reward
QUEENS: 4 gossip, slander — 3 idle gossip — 2 nosy neighbors
JACKS: 4 volatile arguments — 3 friction — 2 slight altercation
TENS: 4 good prospects — 3 serious money problems — 2 small financial gain
NINES: 4 great good fortune — 3 wish fulfilled — 2 pleasant surprise
EIGHTS: 4 anxiety, confusion — 3 worry, stress — 2 love affair
SEVENS: 4 public confrontation — 3 unexpected pregnancy — 2 lies, deceit

YOURSELF: *There is a change ahead which has legal connotations, but it's a good outcome because both the Tens are red.*

YOUR FAMILY: *Three Sevens is news of a birth, but the Seven of Spades suggests that there will be a slight delay.*

YOUR FRIENDS: *Two Eights suggest some mild gossip about a financial issue. Because this position belongs to your friends, the problem is theirs, not yours.*

WHAT YOU EXPECT: *Nine of Hearts is an emotional wish fulfilled, the Eight of Hearts is a celebration about that wish, and the Ace of Diamonds represents either a letter or a ring. Given the other two cards, it would be safe to interpret this card as representing a ring.*

WHAT YOU DON'T EXPECT: *The three Queens show that there is gossip bordering on scandal. But since this position belongs to what you are not expecting to happen, this drama may not be about you, though you will be drawn into it.*

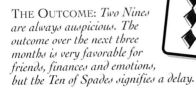

THE OUTCOME: *Two Nines are always auspicious. The outcome over the next three months is very favorable for friends, finances and emotions, but the Ten of Spades signifies a delay.*

Palmistry

For graduates of the psychic workshop, palmistry offers an interesting challenge. Initially they learned to observe the shape of the hands and the lines etched into the palms while they were doing psychometry exercises (holding another student's hands and interpreting the vibrations they received). That is where any thoughts of developing the art of palmistry stopped for all but the students who felt compelled to investigate the meanings of the lines and other signs in the palms.

Should palmistry become your specialty, you should understand that there are just as many complexities to learn as there are in any other psychic discipline. Some lines and symbols appear and disappear on the palms according to the physical and emotional conditions of their owner, and this can be confusing and discouraging to some students.

If you follow the concept that palmistry is a map etched out in the palms of your hands, and compare the main lines — the life line, the heart line, the head line — to the main highways of your journey through life, and the minor lines — marriage, children, health, and travel — to the other roadways on your journey, then the study of palmistry becomes infinitely more interesting and appealing.

Palmistry is not an easy discipline to take on. If you decide to specialize in this craft then you must decide from the beginning to apply yourself with dedication.

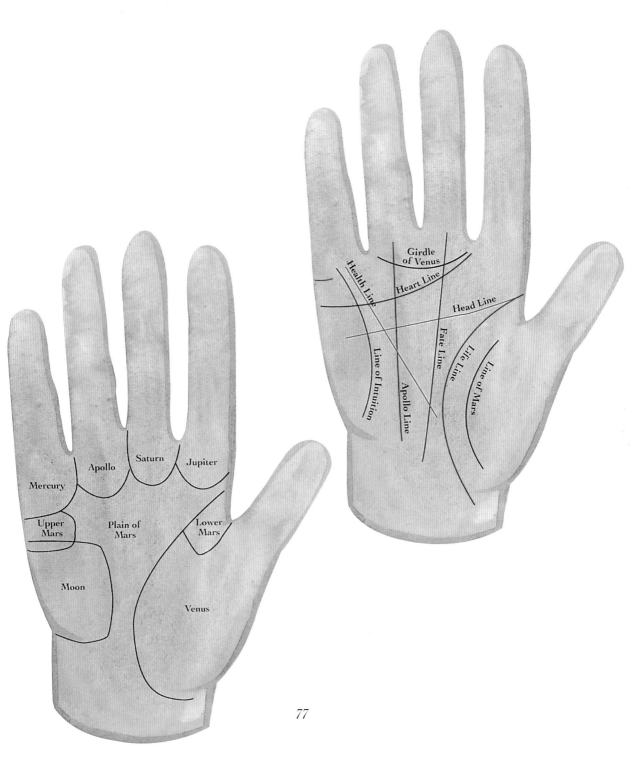

Mercury

Apollo

Saturn

Jupiter

Upper
Mars

Plain of
Mars

Lower
Mars

Moon

Venus

Girdle
of Venus

Health Line

Heart Line

Head Line

Fate Line

Life Line

Line of Mars

Line of Intuition

Apollo Line

CELEBRATING YOUR PSYCHIC GROWTH

WHEN YOU HAVE COMPLETED A PSYCHIC WORKSHOP PROGRAM IN FULL, IT IS CUSTOMARY TO CELEBRATE YOUR NEWFOUND KNOWLEDGE WITH YOUR GROUP BY HAVING A PARTY OR GOING OUT TO DINNER.

It is now time to relax and ponder on the success you have achieved. You have learned the importance of adopting good communication skills and you will notice how you seem to take the time to understand the other person's point of view.

You have given yourself the luxury of knowing that you have expanded all your senses including the important sixth sense which you have decided to trust. You have grown in confidence because you know that you are being the best you can possibly be. You have forgiven yourself for not being perfect. When you began using your psychic ability you switched on a light to which people are attracted, so wherever you go you will find that people will want to befriend you. You have learned how to keep unwanted people away and how to deal with your enemies. You should now know the difference between logic and intuition and how it is possible for these seemingly opposing forces to work together.

You are no longer easily intimidated by challenging circumstances or controlling people. You are proud to have taken control and responsibility for your own life. You know what you will teach your children, how to be proud of who they are, but most importantly, who they can become.

Above all, you have learned that anything is possible if you are prepared to try. You have so much to celebrate, so much to look forward to. Your expectations are high and your attitude is positive. Celebrate your growth with the people you have grown with, and when you have taken that well-deserved break and celebrated enough, maybe it is your turn to teach others the benefit of psychic development in the best way you know how. Start a psychic workshop of your own. Why not? You certainly know how, and you must know you will enjoy the challenge.

Continuing the Growth

You will never be too old to learn more or teach others what you have learned. Everybody knows somebody who wants to develop his or her psychic ability; all you need do is to gather a group of compatible students.

The next step is to test the students' compatibility. Find a suitable workshop and begin to teach what you have practiced. Follow the same rules and guidelines as the ones you observed while a student and you will have yourself a psychic workshop. It is very rewarding to see your students evolve because they are being taught in the right way — your way. Every student of psychic phenomena has something to contribute. As the teacher, you will be surprised how much you are learning from your students.

Returning to the Well

Psychic growth is a continuous process throughout life. Psychic knowledge is like a well that never dries up, to which you can return for replenishment from time to time. Just as the physical body requires nutrition from food, psychic ability needs psychic knowledge to grow and survive. The more you learn, the more you want to learn.

Your contribution to the Well is the psychic energy you generate and give to the universe and the knowledge which you pass on to others for their psychic development. It is within the power of all people to evolve psychically — we own the key to the door of success, we just need to remember how to turn it and set the process in motion.

To Yvonne and Colette
who are now with the angels

© Copyright 1998 Lansdowne Publishing Pty Ltd

This 1999 edition published by Metro Books,
by arrangement with Lansdowne Publishing Pty Ltd

Text: Sylvie Abecassis
Design: Joanna Davies

Metro Books
122 Fifth Avenue
New York, NY 10011

ISBN-13: 978-0-7607-1226-9
ISBN-10: 0-7607-1226-3

Printed and bound in Singapore by Tien Wah Press

14 13 12 11 10 9 8